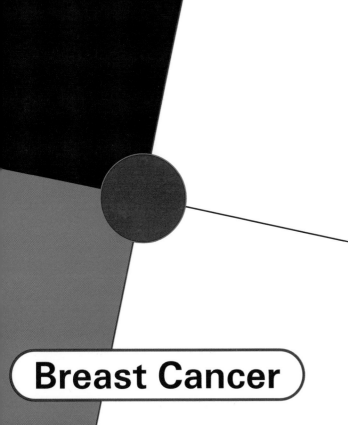

Breast Cancer

By Judith Peacock

Consultant:
Sharol Anderson, BSN, RN, OCN
Breast Health and Oncology Patient Educator
North Memorial Health Care
Robbinsdale, Minnesota

Perspectives on Disease and Illness

LifeMatters
an imprint of Capstone Press
Mankato, Minnesota

LifeMatters books are published by Capstone Press
PO Box 669 • 151 Good Counsel Drive • Mankato, Minnesota 56002
http://www.capstone-press.com

Printed in the United States of America

Library of Congress Cataloging-in-Publication Data
Peacock, Judith, 1942–
    Breast cancer / by Judith Peacock.
        p.   cm. — (Perspectives on disease and illness)
    Includes bibliographical references and index.
    ISBN 0-7368-1028-5
    1. Breast—Cancer—Juvenile literature. [1. Breast—Cancer. 2. Cancer. 3. Diseases.] I. Title.
II. Series.
    RC280 .B8 P325 2002
    616.99′449—dc21   00-012364
                                                     CIP

    Summary: Discusses the types of breast cancer, how breast cancer is diagnosed and treated, how to do breast self-exams, what to expect and how to cope if a mother has breast cancer, and possible future methods of detection and treatment.

Staff Credits
Rebecca Aldridge, editor; Adam Lazar, designer and illustrator; Kim Danger, photo researcher
Interior production by Stacey Field

Photo Credits
Cover: The Stock Market/©Howard Sochurek, bottom; ©Digital Vision, left; ©PhotoDisc/Barbara Penoyar, middle; ©Earthstar Stock, Inc., right
Index Stock Imagery/©Kevin Beebe, 9; ©BSIP Agency, 19, 24, 33; ©Preston Lyon, 23; ©Katie Deits, 32; ©Myrleen Cate, 42; ©Chip Henderson, 47; ©Ken Weingart, 52
International Stock/©Michael Agliolo, 57
Photri, Inc/29
Photo Network/©Henryk T. Kaiser, 10
Unicorn Stock Photos/©Eric R. Berndt, 45
Visuals Unlimited/©Science VU, 6, 37; ©SIU, 27; ©Jeff Greenberg, 38; ©Barry Slaven, 59

A 0 9 8 7 6 5 4 3 2 1

Table of Contents

Chapter Overview

Breast cancer is a major disease among women in the United States and Canada. Thousands of women and hundreds of men die from breast cancer every year.

Breast cancer occurs when abnormal cells in the breast divide uncontrollably and form tumors. Noninvasive, or *in situ*, breast cancer hasn't spread beyond its original location. Invasive breast cancer has spread within the breast or to other areas in the body.

Heredity and radiation are known causes of breast cancer. Poisonous substances in the environment, high levels of estrogen, and a high-fat diet also may cause breast cancer.

Being a woman and getting older pose the biggest risks for developing breast cancer.

Early detection and treatment provide the best hope for surviving breast cancer.

Chapter 1

What Is Breast Cancer?

"I was in seventh grade when my mom was told she had breast cancer. I   **Marty, Age 16**
remember coming home from school and hearing Mom talking on the phone with her sister. Mom was crying and saying that the doctor had found a lump in her breast. I got really scared. I wondered, 'Is Mom going to die?'"

It's hard to avoid hearing or thinking about breast cancer. Newspapers, magazines, and TV shows feature stories on breast cancer almost every day. Many people know someone who has breast cancer. The person they know might be a mother, grandmother, aunt, sister, or family friend. A lot of people also know someone who has died from this disease.

The breast pictured on the left is normal. The breast on the right is cancerous.

What Is Breast Cancer?

The word *cancer* refers to more than 100 related diseases. Cancer can affect every part of the body. Cancer that begins in the breast is called breast cancer.

Cancer involves the cells of the body. In a healthy body, cells grow, divide, and produce new cells as needed. Sometimes something goes wrong with this process. Cells keep dividing and produce more cells than the body needs. The extra cells form a mass known as a growth or tumor. The tumor may be a lump or a thickening of body tissue.

There are two types of tumors. Benign tumors are not cancer. They can be removed and usually don't grow back. They don't spread and don't threaten a person's life. Malignant tumors, on the other hand, are cancer. The cells are abnormal. These unusual cells divide without control and can penetrate and destroy healthy tissue around them. They can break away and travel to other parts of the body where they start new tumors. Malignant tumors can be life threatening.

Fast Fact

Breast cancer is the second-leading cause of cancer deaths among U.S. women. Lung cancer is first with 67,600 deaths expected in 2000.

Noninvasive and Invasive Breast Cancer

Breast cancer may be noninvasive or invasive. Noninvasive means the cancer hasn't spread beyond its original location. It's *in situ*, or "in place." Invasive breast cancer has made its way out of its original location. It has spread farther into the breast or outside the breast. Invasive breast cancer can be more difficult to treat than noninvasive breast cancer.

What Causes Breast Cancer?

There may be several causes of breast cancer. Two well-established factors are heredity and radiation. Heredity is the passing on of traits from parents to children through genes. Radiation is particles sent out from radioactive substances. Scientists also suspect that the environment, estrogen, and people's diet may have something to do with the disease. Estrogen is a female sex hormone that affects body development.

Heredity

Being born with mutated, or damaged, breast cancer genes causes from 5 to 10 percent of breast cancer cases. Genes are the material in cells that determine a person's characteristics. The breast cancer genes Breast Cancer 1 (BRCA 1) and Breast Cancer 2 (BRCA 2) are supposed to stop tumor growth. When these genes are abnormal, they can't carry out their function.

Radiation

Exposure to high doses of ionizing, or electrically charging, radiation has been proven to increase cancer risk. This exposure especially can affect women younger than 30. Studies show high cancer rates among survivors of atomic bomb explosions. Studies also show high rates for people who work in uranium mines.

Myth: Getting hit in the breasts or having your breasts fondled, or touched lovingly, causes breast cancer.

Fact: Like all cancers, breast cancer is caused by abnormal cells that grow out of control.

Environment

Chemicals used in factories and on farms and chemicals in everyday household products may cause breast cancer. Pesticides for killing bugs, as well as fuels, plastics, detergents, and other poisonous substances may damage breast cancer genes. These chemicals haven't been proven to cause breast cancer. However, studies are currently being done to determine their effect.

Researchers have found higher rates of breast cancer in areas with heavy industry, such as the northeastern United States. The United States, Canada, and other developed countries have more breast cancer than less developed countries. Breast cancer rates are increasing in areas of the world undergoing rapid industrial growth.

Estrogen

Estrogen is a female hormone produced by the ovaries, which are female sex organs. Hormones control body growth and functions. Estrogen triggers breast development and helps regulate the menstrual cycle. This is the time from one menstruation to the next. Menstruation is a female's period, her monthly loss of blood, fluid, and tissue. Estrogen increases the number of cells in the breasts during menstruation. It also may stimulate the growth of breast cancer cells.

Diet

A high-fat diet may contribute to breast cancer by raising estrogen levels in the body. As possible evidence, researchers point to Japan, a developed country where the rate of breast cancer is quite low. Women in Japan typically eat less fat than women in the United States and Canada do.

Pesticides sprayed on crops may be one environmental cause of breast cancer.

Who Gets Breast Cancer?

Breast cancer can develop in anyone, but the biggest risk factors are being female and aging. The majority of breast cancer cases occur in women older than 50.

Additional Risk Factors for Breast Cancer

Besides sex and age, the following factors may put a woman at risk for breast cancer. Even so, from 75 to 80 percent of women with breast cancer have none of these risk factors.

Has family or personal history of breast cancer. A woman whose grandmother, mother, or sister has had breast cancer is at risk. If more than one close relative has had the disease, the risk increases. A woman who has had breast cancer in the past is at risk of getting it again.

Has long menstrual history. A woman whose periods began at age 12 or earlier and ended past age 50 is at risk. A long menstrual history means more exposure to estrogen.

Never had a baby or had first child after age 30. Pregnancy is thought to protect cells from estrogen. Delaying pregnancy until after age 30 increases exposure to estrogen.

Studies also have linked breast cancer to other factors. These include lack of exercise, being overweight, smoking, and drinking two or more drinks of alcohol daily. Long-term use of birth control pills may be another risk factor.

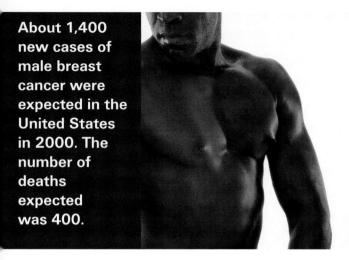

About 1,400 new cases of male breast cancer were expected in the United States in 2000. The number of deaths expected was 400.

Race and Breast Cancer

Breast cancer is more common among Caucasian women than among African American women. However, more African American women die of breast cancer than Caucasian women do. The higher death rate among African American women may be due to higher poverty levels and lack of knowledge about breast cancer. Some researchers suggest that African American women may be subject to a more rapidly growing form of breast cancer.

Income Level and Breast Cancer

Income level affects a woman's chances of surviving breast cancer. Women with low income often lack access to medical care. They may delay treatment until tumors become large and difficult to treat. Women with higher income tend to have regular medical checkups. Their cancer is more likely to be caught early.

Men and Breast Cancer

Men, as well as women, can have breast cancer. Male breast cancer accounts for about 1 percent of all breast cancers. Risk factors for men include growing older, a family history of breast cancer, and enlarged breasts. Many people think of breast cancer as a "woman's" disease. Therefore, men with breast cancer may be embarrassed to seek treatment.

One study showed that 61 percent of women fear breast cancer, while 9 percent fear heart disease. However, heart disease, not breast cancer, is the number one killer of women in the United States.

Surviving Breast Cancer

Much more needs to be learned about the causes of breast cancer. Doctors do know, however, that detecting and treating breast cancer in its early stages can save lives. Women whose cancer is confined to the breast have a 96 percent chance of surviving five years after diagnosis. Women whose cancer has spread to distant parts of the body have a lower survival rate. They have only a 21 percent chance of surviving five years after diagnosis. Almost 60 percent of women with breast cancer survive 15 years after diagnosis.

A Frightening Disease

The thought of having breast cancer terrifies most people. There's fear of being sick and in pain. There's fear of losing a breast and being disfigured, or losing attractiveness. There's the possibility of death. Breast cancer can be frightening, but knowing the facts about this disease can take away some of the fear.

Points to Consider

Why do a woman's chances for breast cancer increase as she gets older?

Why do you think most people are more afraid of breast cancer than they are of heart disease?

How do you think it would feel to be told you had breast cancer? Explain.

Chapter Overview

The female breast consists of lobules, or glands, that produce milk and ducts that deliver milk to the nipple.

Almost all breast cancers begin in either the ducts or the lobes. Ductal cancer and lobular cancer can be invasive or noninvasive. Two other types of breast cancer are inflammatory breast cancer and Paget's disease.

Breast cancer can be divided into five stages. Each stage indicates how large the tumor is and how far it has spread. Breast cancer is treated most successfully in the early stages.

Many conditions other than cancer can affect the breast. Benign breast problems may cause pain and discomfort, but they usually can be treated successfully.

Chapter 2

Types of Breast Cancer

Breast cancer is a complicated disease. Several different types exist, and a woman can have more than one type at a time. Many other breast problems exist that are not cancer. Distinguishing between benign breast problems and cancer can be difficult. Benign problems usually can be treated successfully.

Inside the Female Breast

Human beings belong to the class of animals known as mammals. One characteristic of mammals is that the female nurses her young. That means she feeds her baby milk from her breast. In human beings, the female breasts are mammary, or milk-producing, organs. Knowing about the internal structure of the breast helps to understand breast cancer.

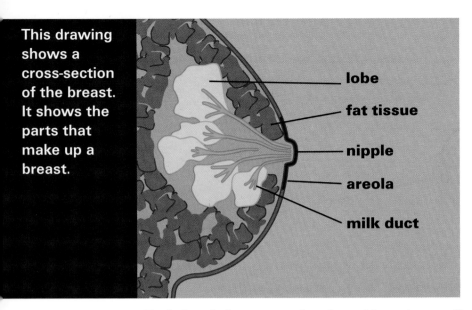

This drawing shows a cross-section of the breast. It shows the parts that make up a breast.

lobe

fat tissue

nipple

areola

milk duct

Each female breast contains about 20 sections, called lobes. The lobes are arranged in a circle like the sections of an orange. Each lobe contains many smaller lobules, which end in dozens of tiny milk-producing glands. Ducts, or narrow tubes, carry the milk out to the nipple. This is the tip of the breast. Fatty tissue fills the space between and around the ducts and lobes. The fatty tissue makes the breast feel soft.

The breast also contains blood vessels, nerves, and small muscles. In addition, there are vessels that carry lymph. This is a clear liquid that contains infection-fighting white blood cells. The lymph system runs throughout the body. Small, bean-shaped organs called lymph nodes are located along the lymph system. There are lymph nodes underneath the arm.

Two Main Types of Breast Cancer

Two main types of breast cancer are ductal carcinoma and lobular carcinoma. (*Carcinoma* is another word for "cancer.") Ductal carcinoma is found in the lining of the milk ducts. Lobular carcinoma is found in the lobules. Both types may be called adenocarcinoma of the breast. Both types can be invasive or noninvasive (*in situ*).

Male breasts contain undeveloped milk ducts beneath the areola and nipple. The areola is the colored ring around the nipple. Most male breast cancer first appears as a small, hard, painless lump in the nipple area. The types of breast cancer found in men are similar to those found in women. Men may have IDC, DCIS, inflammatory breast cancer, and Paget's disease. LCIS has not been seen in men.

Ductal Carcinoma *In Situ* (DCIS)

This is the most common type of noninvasive cancer. It hasn't spread beyond the duct in which it's located. DCIS often is called a precancer condition. It consists of abnormal cells that could become invasive. Instead of balling up into lumps, DCIS cells fan out along the milk duct. DCIS appears on a mammogram, or special X ray, as tiny specks of calcium. Improvements in mammography have resulted in many more cases of DCIS being diagnosed.

Lobular Carcinoma *In Situ* (LCIS)

This type also is considered a precancer condition. A mammogram rarely shows LCIS. This type of cancer usually is discovered while another breast lump is being examined.

Invasive Ductal Carcinoma (IDC)

This type accounts for about 70 percent of invasive breast cancers. It's the most common cause of a lump that can be felt. IDC may cause changes in the skin, such as dimpling or puckering. It also may cause the nipple to retract, or pull in.

Invasive Lobular Carcinoma (ILC)

This type is more a thickening of breast tissue than a lump. It usually is discovered after a tissue sample has been removed from the breast. ILC accounts for about 10 percent of invasive breast cancers.

Myth: Only women with large breasts get breast cancer.

Fact: Cancer can develop in any size breasts.

Other Types of Breast Cancer

Two other types of breast cancer are inflammatory breast cancer and Paget's disease. Inflammatory breast cancer causes the breast to appear red and feel warm. Paget's disease affects the nipple. The tumor grows from ducts beneath the nipple onto the surface of the nipple.

Stages of Breast Cancer

Like other cancers, breast cancer is classified by stages. The stages indicate the size of the tumor and how far the cancer has spread. Breast cancer has five stages. It is treated most successfully in the early stages.

Stage 0. This is noninvasive breast cancer. The cancer cells haven't gone beyond the ducts or lobules.

Stage 1. The tumor is still within the breast. It's 2 centimeters (about ¾ inch) or less in diameter.

Stage 2. The tumor is larger than 2 centimeters but smaller than 5 centimeters (2 inches). The lymph nodes under the arm test positive for cancer.

Stages 3A and 3B. In stage 3A, the tumor is larger than 5 centimeters and spreads to the lymph nodes under the arm. In stage 3B, the tumor spreads to the skin, chest wall, or lymph nodes near the sternum, or breastbone.

Stage 4. Cancer cells break away from the tumor. The lymph system and bloodstream carry them to other parts of the body. Cancer cells may be carried to places such as the bones, liver, lungs, or brain. The spread of cancer from the original tumor to other body parts is called metastasis.

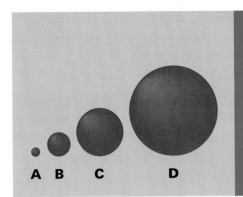

Average size of lump found by (A) early mammograms (B) first mammogram (C) woman doing monthly breast self-exams (D) woman doing occasional breast self-exams.

A B C D

"I knew my mother's tumor was only a clump of cells, but I imagined it to be an evil octopus. Its tentacles grew and multiplied and wrapped themselves around every part of her body. The monster hissed and laughed at my mother's pain. I felt helpless to stop it."

Camille, Age 15

Common Benign Breast Problems

Menstruation and several conditions other than cancer can affect the breast. These conditions include benign lumps, infections, and nipple discharge. Benign breast problems usually can be treated successfully.

Cyclic Changes

A woman's menstrual cycle may cause temporary changes in her breasts. They may swell and feel tender and painful before and during her periods. The breasts tend to change because of changing hormones. This is normal.

General Lumpiness

Many women have naturally lumpy breasts or fibrocystic changes. Their breasts may feel like rope or partially cooked grains of rice. Their breasts may feel this way especially around the nipple or upper part of the breast.

Did You Know?

At one time, the term *fibrocystic disease* was a general name for a variety of benign breast conditions. Doctors used it to describe conditions such as lumpy breasts, breast pain, and nipple discharge. Most doctors no longer use this term. Hearing the word *disease* frightened women into thinking they were sick or at risk of getting sick. Many women with this diagnosis had difficulty getting health insurance. A health care provider may say that you or someone you know has fibrocystic disease. If this happens, ask for the specific name of the condition.

Single Lumps

Several types of benign lumps exist.

Cysts are sacs filled with a muddy-looking fluid. They can grow large and cause pain. Cysts are the most common cause of lumps in women age 30 to 50.

Fibroadenomas feel solid, round, and rubbery and can be moved around easily. These are the most common type of tumor in women in their late teens and early 20s.

Fat necrosis consists of damaged or disintegrating fatty tissue. It often develops as a result of a bruise or a blow to the breasts.

Sclerosing adenosis is excessive growth of tissue in the lobules. This can be hard to distinguish from cancer.

Infection

The breasts may become infected. The skin looks red and feels hot and swollen. A blocked milk duct can be one cause of infection.

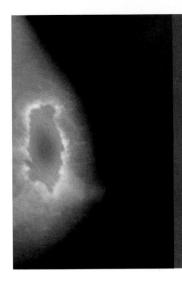

This sonogram (see page 26) shows a breast cyst. A cyst is a benign lump that can become large and painful.

Nipple Discharge

Fluid may come out of the nipple. This discharge may be caused by another breast condition such as lumpiness or infection. It may be a side effect of medication. A clear, greenish, or milky discharge usually is benign.

Hyperplasia and Atypia

Most benign conditions don't turn into cancer. Hyperplasia and atypia are exceptions. Hyperplasia means there are too many cells in a duct. Atypia means there are too many cells, plus the cells are becoming abnormal. These conditions slightly increase a woman's chances of breast cancer. It's sometimes difficult to tell the difference between DCIS and atypia.

Points to Consider

Do you know someone who has breast cancer? What type and stage of breast cancer does this person have?

Why is it important for males and teens to know about breast cancer?

How can knowing about benign breast conditions help a woman and her family?

Chapter Overview

The discovery of a lump or mass in the breast usually begins the process for diagnosing cancer. A tumor may change the breast in ways that can be seen.

Signs and symptoms of breast cancer are similar to those of many benign breast conditions. Most lumps are not cancer.

Regular breast self-exams, clinical exams, and mammograms are important for breast cancer detection.

A mammogram can detect an abnormal area in the breast long before it can be felt. Early detection increases the chances for survival and gives a woman more choices for treatment. Mammograms don't detect all cancers. They have limited benefit for younger women whose breast tissue tends to be dense.

Ultrasound is another tool for examining the breast.

A biopsy is the only way to tell for sure if a tumor is cancer. Two kinds of biopsy are needle biopsy and surgical biopsy.

Chapter 3

Diagnosing Breast Cancer

A diagnosis of cancer usually begins with the discovery of a lump in the breast. The woman herself might discover the lump during a routine breast self-exam. A health care professional might feel the lump during a clinical breast exam. The lump might be discovered on a mammogram.

Signs and Symptoms of Breast Cancer

A lump or mass that can be seen or felt is the best-known sign of breast cancer. The following page lists other warning signs and symptoms of breast cancer. These may be present whether or not a lump can be seen or felt.

Did You Know?

Men, too, should do a breast self-exam each month. They should report any changes in their chest or breast area to their doctor. Unfortunately, no screening test for male breast cancer exists.

Change in the breast's skin color or texture. The skin might appear red. Enlarged pores can make the skin's texture look like an orange peel.

Depression or dimpling of the skin. The tumor may be pulling the skin in to create a hollow.

Change in the direction in which the nipple points. The nipple might become an "innie" when it used to stick out.

Change in the size or shape of the breast. The breast might have grown or gotten smaller. It might have developed a bulge or a dip.

Rash on the breast skin or a sore on the nipple.

Bloody discharge from the nipple or spontaneous fluid of any color. Spontaneous means the discharge appears without squeezing the nipple.

Breast pain, tenderness, or swelling not related to the menstrual cycle.

The symptoms on this list may be symptoms of other breast diseases and conditions, as well. In fact, 80 percent of breast problems are not cancerous. It's important, however, to report any unusual changes in breast health to a doctor immediately. Even if the condition is benign, it still may need treatment.

A breast self-exam is a specific way of checking the breast for lumps or changes.

The Big Three

At the present time, early detection offers the best defense against breast cancer. The American Cancer Society recommends the following:

Breast self-exam (BSE). All women age 20 and older should do a BSE each month. (Chapter 6 explains how to do a BSE.)

Clinical breast exam. Women age 20 through 39 should have a breast exam by a health care professional every three years. Women age 40 and older should have their breasts examined every year.

Mammogram. Women age 40 and older should have a mammogram every year. This is a special low-dose X ray that shows the inside of the breast.

Clinical Breast Exam

A clinical breast exam means that a health care professional examines a woman's breasts. The exam might be part of a regular checkup, or it might take place after a woman has discovered a lump. A nurse, doctor, or gynecologist conducts the exam. A gynecologist is a doctor who specializes in the female reproductive system. The health care professional examines the woman's breasts visually. He or she feels under the armpits and feels the breast tissue in a specific and orderly way. Depending on the exam's results, the health care professional may recommend further testing.

A mammogram is one of the best tools currently available for finding breast cancer early.

Mammogram

Mammography can identify a tumor when it's still too tiny to be felt. Mammograms are used in two ways. They are used to screen for breast cancer before any symptoms appear. They're also used to diagnose breast cancer when symptoms are present. Mammograms use only a small amount of radiation and aren't harmful to most people.

What Happens During a Mammogram?

A special X-ray machine is used to perform mammography. First, the woman removes all clothing above the waist. Then, a technician, or person trained to perform mammograms, places the woman's breast on a small platform. The breast is squeezed and flattened by a plastic shield to get a clearer image. The woman must hold her breath while the X-ray film is exposed. Then the technician repositions the machine and takes another image. Two or three images are made of each breast.

The mammogram may be diagnostic, or used for diagnosis of an existing lump. If so, the technician spends more time and takes additional views. He or she may use a special cone to compress the spot in question. This makes seeing the lump easier.

Breast Cancer

Did You Know?

Both mammography and physical examination of the breasts are important. Breast cancer cells may take 10 years to become a tumor large enough to be seen on a mammogram. It may take a few more years before the tumor can be felt during a physical examination. Breast self-exams may detect a fast-growing tumor.

A radiologist studies the X rays for anything abnormal. A radiologist is a doctor who specializes in diagnosis using X rays and other imaging tools. He or she compares the woman's new X-ray films to her old films. That way the radiologist can see if there have been any changes. If a lump is present, the radiologist examines the mammogram for other possible areas of cancer. The radiologist then sends a report to the woman's doctor. More and more clinics, however, are reading mammograms and giving the results during the woman's appointment. This helps to relieve anxiety for the woman and her loved ones.

Advantages and Disadvantages

At the present time, mammograms are the best tool available for early detection of breast cancer. Even so, they have disadvantages. Mammograms aren't able to detect all breast cancers. They only X-ray the part of the breast that sticks out. That means they may miss tumors growing along the chest wall. Mammograms are less precise for younger women than for older women. The younger a woman is the denser her breasts are. Dense breast tissue makes seeing what is actually there more difficult.

Another disadvantage is that mammograms can be expensive. Many women don't have health insurance that covers the cost of mammograms. These women may be unable to pay for X rays themselves. Mammograms should be done in a facility that specializes in mammography or conducts many mammograms a day. This helps to ensure a high standard of safety and quality. Many women live in an area where such a facility is not available.

Mammograms fail to detect breast cancer **20** percent of the time in women older than **50**. These tests may fail as much as **40** percent of the time in younger women.

Who Should Have a Mammogram and How Often?

Breast cancer experts disagree on whether screening mammograms should start at age 40 or age 50. They also disagree on whether a woman should have a mammogram every year or every other year. The American Cancer Society, the National Cancer Institute, and several other breast cancer groups do agree on screening mammograms. These organizations recommend that every woman age 40 and older have a screening mammogram every year. These organizations know that sometimes mammograms create false alarms for women age 40 to 49. However, these organizations believe that it still is better to check out a possible tumor than to leave it untested.

For women younger than 40, mammograms are recommended for only a few reasons. They may be used to diagnose a suspicious growth. Mammograms also are recommended if a woman has a personal or family history of breast cancer. Some doctors suggest a baseline, or first, mammogram for healthy women at age 35. Doctors then have an image of the healthy breast with which to compare future mammograms.

Ultrasound

An ultrasound, or sonogram, is another valuable tool for seeing inside the breast. It creates images using sound waves. Ultrasound usually is ordered as a follow-up to a mammogram. It can help interpret a mammogram or provide additional information. Ultrasound is valuable especially for telling whether a lump is fluid-filled (a cyst) or solid. It may be the first test for a younger woman or a woman known to have dense breasts.

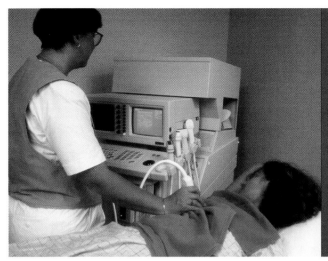

An ultrasound may be the first test used to detect breast cancer in a young woman. It also may be the first test for a woman who is known to have dense breasts.

"One morning I woke up and my chest hurt. I thought it was because I slept the wrong way or because I was getting my period. I did a breast exam and found a lump in my left breast.

Luz, Age 15

"My mother took me to see her gynecologist. The doctor didn't think the lump was anything serious, but he thought that maybe I should have an ultrasound. I was really scared about what the lump might be. I knew one of the possibilities was cancer.

"I had the ultrasound on a Wednesday morning. I had just gotten home when a surgeon called my house. She said I had a mass in my breast that was one and a half inches in diameter. It had to be removed right away. The news made me even more scared.

"By Friday morning, I was in surgery. The surgeon didn't think I had cancer, but surgery was the only sure way to tell. A week later, the results came back negative. I didn't have cancer. Instead, the surgeon said it was something called a fibroadenoma. I was so relieved and happy. You just can't imagine.

"I still do breast exams. I tell my friends they should do them, too. If a lump could happen to me, it could happen to anyone."

Myth: One in eight women will get breast cancer.

Fact: This often-quoted statement really means risk over a lifetime. Risk goes up with age. For example, a woman who reaches the age of 50 has a 1 in 52 chance of getting breast cancer. A woman who reaches the age of 90 has a one in eight chance of getting breast cancer.

Biopsy

If something suspicious appears on a mammogram or during a clinical breast exam, a biopsy is performed. During a biopsy, a breast surgeon removes a sample of tissue or an entire lump from the breast. The tissue is then examined under a microscope. A biopsy is the only way to tell for sure if a tumor is cancerous.

Two main types of biopsy are needle biopsy and surgical biopsy. The procedure used depends on several things, including the lump's location. A needle biopsy can be done in a surgeon's or a radiologist's office. A surgical biopsy usually requires a hospital operating room.

Needle Biopsy

There are several types of needle biopsy.

Fine needle biopsy. The surgeon uses a small needle and syringe to remove fluid or a sample of cells. A syringe is a tube with a plunger.

Core needle biopsy. The surgeon uses a larger needle to remove tissue. Ultrasound may be used to locate the lump or guide the needle.

Stereotactic biopsy. The woman lies on a special table that has an opening for her breast to hang through. The breast is compressed, and two mammograms are taken at once. This creates a 3-D image to guide the needle.

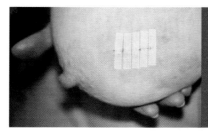

After an incision is made for a biopsy, it's closed up with stitches.

Surgical Biopsy

There are two types of surgical biopsy.

Incisional surgical biopsy. This method is used when a tumor is large. The surgeon cuts open the breast to remove a sample. Then, he or she closes this incision with stitches.

Excisional surgical biopsy. The surgeon removes the entire lump and some of the tissue around it.

Other Diagnostic Tests

Doctors may use other tests to see if the cancer has spread beyond the breasts. A chest X ray will show if the cancer is in the lungs. Blood tests will indicate if the cancer has invaded vital organs such as the liver, stomach, or colon. These tests usually aren't necessary if the cancer is caught in the early stages.

Points to Consider

Why is a patient's medical history important in diagnosing breast cancer?

Ask a relative who has had a mammogram to describe the procedure.

Imagine that your grandmother says to you, "I'm 65 years old. Why should I have a mammogram?" How would you respond?

Are there any programs in your community that help women with low income get regular mammograms? How could you find out?

Chapter Overview

The goal of breast cancer treatment is to remove or kill cancer cells so that the disease can't spread. Treatment plans vary from woman to woman.

Lumpectomy and mastectomy are two types of surgery. A lumpectomy is removal of only the tumor. A mastectomy is removal of the entire breast.

Chemotherapy treats the cancer with strong drugs. Many women undergoing chemotherapy experience unpleasant side effects. Radiation therapy uses high-energy X rays to kill cancer cells in the area of the tumor. Hormone therapy prevents estrogen from stimulating the growth of cancer cells. It works throughout the body.

Complementary therapy goes along with traditional methods. It helps people undergoing traditional methods feel better. Alternative therapy replaces traditional methods.

No cure for breast cancer exists. However, doctors often say a woman is cured if she is free of cancer five years following treatment.

Chapter 4

Treatment for Breast Cancer

The goal of treatment for breast cancer is to remove or kill cancer cells so that the disease can't spread. Treatment varies from woman to woman. It depends on the size and type of tumor and on whether the tumor has metastasized. Doctors also consider the woman's age, medical history, and personal preferences. Traditional treatment methods include surgery, chemotherapy, radiation therapy, and hormone therapy. These methods are described in the following paragraphs. Doctors may use a combination of two or more treatment methods.

Surgery

Surgery to remove the tumor usually is the first step in breast cancer treatment. The two main types of surgery are lumpectomy and mastectomy. The ending *-ectomy* means "to cut."

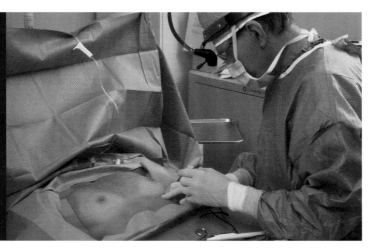

Lumpectomy

In a lumpectomy, surgeons remove the malignant tumor. They also remove a small amount of tissue from around the tumor to make sure no cancer remains. This type of surgery sometimes is called "breast-conserving surgery." Surgeons try to save as much of the breast as possible. After the operation, the woman will have a scar and perhaps a small dent in her breast. Radiation therapy often is used as a follow-up treatment for a lumpectomy.

Mastectomy

In a mastectomy, surgeons remove the entire breast. A double mastectomy is removal of both breasts. A mastectomy might be simple, radical, or modified radical, depending on how much additional tissue is removed. Mastectomy is used less often these days than in the past. Doctors may use lumpectomy followed by radiation therapy instead. This combination usually can be as effective as a mastectomy in preventing the spread of cancer.

Some women who are at high risk for breast cancer choose preventive mastectomy. A preventive mastectomy is the removal of a woman's breasts before cancer even has a chance to begin. Women who decide on this surgery usually have a grandmother, mother, and one or more sisters with breast cancer. This makes these women likely targets for the disease, too.

After a mastectomy, the woman has a scar on her chest. Some women choose to have breast reconstruction. A plastic surgeon may build a new breast using tissue from other parts of the woman's body. Or, the surgeon may use silicone or saline implants that are placed under the skin. Other women choose to wear a prosthesis, which is an artificial breast form. It's worn in or under clothing and helps to create a natural-looking breast. Still other women choose neither to use a prosthesis nor have reconstruction.

Complications From Breast Surgery

Surgery for breast cancer can cause difficult aftereffects. The woman may lose arm and shoulder strength and experience numbness from having muscles and nerves cut. She may feel lopsided, or out of balance, with only one breast.

Ten to twelve percent of women who have breast surgery develop lymphedema. This can be one of the most troublesome aftereffects. Surgeons generally remove lymph nodes from under the arm to determine if the cancer has spread. The number of lymph nodes removed varies from person to person. Anywhere between 1 to 30 or more nodes might be removed. Fluid that would normally flow through the lymph nodes collects in the chest, arm, and hand. This causes them to swell to two or three times their normal size. Lymphedema can be painful and unattractive.

The trend in breast cancer treatment is to invade a woman's body as little as possible. This means not doing a mastectomy when a lumpectomy would do just as well. It means not doing a surgical biopsy when a needle biopsy would be just as good. This noninvasive approach helps to make breast cancer treatment less shocking and upsetting for a woman.

Chemotherapy

Chemotherapy consists of strong drugs used to kill cancer cells throughout the body. It usually is a follow-up treatment to surgery. However, chemotherapy can be used before surgery to shrink large tumors. In some instances, chemotherapy may be used by itself.

Researchers have found that using more than one type of chemotherapy drug works best. The woman's oncologist decides on the type and combination of drugs to use. This doctor, who specializes in cancer, also decides the dosage and the frequency for taking the drugs.

What Happens During Chemotherapy

Chemotherapy drugs are taken in pill form or through an intravenous (IV) injection, or shot. For intravenous chemotherapy, the woman usually goes to her doctor's office or an outpatient clinic. There, a nurse inserts a hollow needle into a vein in the woman's arm. The needle is attached to a long tube that is attached to a bag containing the drugs. Through the tube and needle, the drugs slowly drip into the woman's body. A chemotherapy treatment can last from one to six hours.

Some women receive their medication through a port. This is a device installed in a larger vein. A port delivers the drugs continuously into the bloodstream. A port is used when the veins of a woman's arm already have been used a lot. One also may be used when a woman can't tolerate the usual IV treatment.

Treatment for male breast cancer is the same as that for female breast cancer. It usually includes a combination of surgery, radiation, chemotherapy, and/or hormone therapy.

Side Effects of Chemotherapy

Chemotherapy can produce unpleasant side effects. The drugs attack not only cancer cells but also healthy cells. These include hair follicle cells, cells lining the digestive tract, red blood cells, and disease-fighting white blood cells. As a result, a person undergoing chemotherapy may lose her hair. She may feel nauseous, or the need to throw up. She may vomit, or throw up, frequently. Food may lose its taste, and the woman won't feel like eating. She may be tired much of the time and pick up infections easily.

The side effects of chemotherapy can make a person feel miserable. However, there are many ways to control and manage these side effects. For example, some prescription drugs can help reduce nausea from chemotherapy or help stimulate the appetite. Also, side effects usually go away once treatment is completed.

"My grandma and I get along great. We joke around a lot. Nothing seems to get her down. I was shocked when I saw how she looked after chemo. Her head was completely bald. I didn't want to make her feel bad, so I just grinned and said, 'Gosh, Grandma, who's your barber?' She really got a good laugh out of that."

Ethan, Age 14

Dr. Jerri Nielsen served as camp physician at an American research base in Antarctica. In June 1999, during her service, she discovered a lump in her breast. Dr. Nielsen performed a biopsy on herself after practicing on a yam. She sent digital images of the tumor cells to doctors in the United States. Because it was winter at the South Pole, Dr. Nielsen couldn't be rescued for four months. She was forced to treat herself with chemotherapy drugs that were parachuted to the Pole in July. Dr. Nielsen eventually was rescued and continued treatment in the United States.

Radiation Therapy

Like surgery, radiation therapy targets cancer cells inside the breast. It may be used before surgery to shrink tumors or after surgery to kill any remaining cancer cells. In external radiation therapy, a machine directs high-energy X rays in the area of the tumor. The woman may receive small amounts of radiation five days a week for six to seven weeks. Each treatment lasts only a minute or two. Internal radiation therapy involves placing plastic tubes of radioactive material inside the breast. The woman usually must remain in the hospital while being treated.

Radiation therapy can have some side effects. Fatigue, or tiredness, is one side effect. Also, the skin may become red, irritated, and dry in the treatment area. Usually, the skin heals after therapy is completed.

Hormone Therapy

Hormone therapy seeks to prevent estrogen from stimulating the growth of cancer cells. It can be done through surgery to remove the ovaries. Another way to do hormone therapy is through the use of radiation to keep the ovaries from producing estrogen. Drugs that block the body's use of estrogen are another kind of hormone therapy.

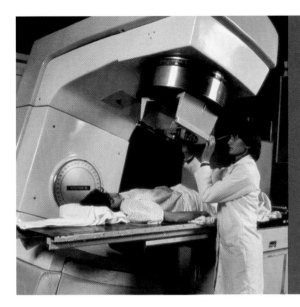

External radiation therapy is one type of breast cancer treatment.

Tamoxifen is a well-known drug used in hormone therapy. Side effects of tamoxifen may include hot flashes, irregular periods, vaginal discharge or dryness, and weight gain. Some researchers believe tamoxifen may increase a woman's chance of getting uterine cancer. This is cancer of the uterus, the organ where an unborn baby grows and develops. Tamoxifen also may slightly increase a woman's risk of developing cataracts. This is a clouding of the eye that results in poor vision. Most women tolerate tamoxifen well.

"My mother was diagnosed with ductal carcinoma *in situ*. Three sites were found. My mom did monthly breast self-exams. But because the tumors were so small and so deep in her breast, she couldn't feel them. Mom says that without mammography her tumors would've been much larger by the time she found them through examination. If that had been the case, her surgery and treatment would have been much harder. Luckily, Mom was able to have a lumpectomy, followed by six weeks of radiation. She also takes tamoxifen."

Nichele, Age 18

Meditation for relaxation is one example of complementary therapy.

Complementary and Alternative Therapy

Two other kinds of therapies are complementary therapy and alternative therapy. Complementary therapy goes along with and supports traditional therapy. It "completes" traditional therapy by helping the person with breast cancer feel better. Examples of complementary therapy include the following:

Exercise programs to help a woman regain strength and ability to move after surgery

Relaxation techniques to help a woman cope with chemotherapy

Programs that teach a woman how to manage lymphedema

Programs that provide wigs or prosthetic devices or show a woman how to look her best

Alternative therapy, on the other hand, takes the place of traditional methods. Instead of surgery followed by chemotherapy, a woman with breast cancer might go on a special diet. She might take vitamins or eat certain herbs. She might take a drug that hasn't been approved by the government. People with cancer often choose alternative therapy when traditional methods have been unsuccessful for them. Alternative therapies must be selected with care. While some alternative therapies might help, some also can be dangerous.

More and more women are surviving breast cancer—thanks to early detection and better treatment methods. Here are some well-known cancer survivors:

Olivia Newton-John, singer
Linda Ellerbee, reporter
Carly Simon, singer
Kate Jackson, actress
Betty Ford, former first lady
Sandra Day O'Connor, supreme court justice
Peggy Fleming, ice skater

Breast Cancer Recurrence

At the present time, no cure for breast cancer exists. Many doctors say that a woman is cured if she is free of cancer five years after treatment. A woman who has had breast cancer always must be on guard for its return. This means continuing to do monthly breast self-exams and having regular clinical breast exams and mammograms. The possibility that the cancer can return is a constant worry. However, knowing that breast cancer can be beaten may give a woman and her family confidence and hope.

Points to Consider

What might be some advantages and disadvantages of each type of treatment for breast cancer?

Do you know anyone who has been treated for breast cancer? If so, what did the person's treatment plan involve?

How could you help a woman undergoing chemotherapy?

Have you heard about breast cancer treatments that seem too good to be true? Describe them.

Chapter Overview

Breast cancer can disturb family life and create tension among family members. At the same time, dealing with breast cancer can bring a family closer together.

Individuals and families can learn to cope with breast cancer. Many resources are available to help families deal with breast cancer. Families shouldn't try to deal with the effects of this illness on their own.

Breast cancer affects a woman's emotions as well as her body. It can make her feel depressed, anxious, and upset.

Teens don't have the power to make their mother well, but they can make her feel more comfortable.

Losing a mother to breast cancer can be extremely difficult for a teen.

Chapter 5

If Your Mother Has Breast Cancer

Breast Cancer and Family Members

If a mother has breast cancer, everyone in the family is affected. If she is recovering from surgery or undergoing treatment, she may be unable to help her family. Jobs such as laundry, cooking, and cleaning may not get done, or they may not be done as well. A single mother may have no one to get the kids off to school when she has treatment. Children may have no one to help them with homework or drive them to soccer practice. There may be less money to pay bills if the mother can't go to work.

When a mother is diagnosed with breast cancer, a teen may need to take on more responsibilities at home.

Everyone in the family usually worries about the mother and wonders if she'll get better. Family members may be angry that their life has been upset. Children may believe they caused their mother's illness and feel guilty. They may feel neglected if their father must spend time caring for their mother. Feelings of worry, fear, anger, and guilt can create tension in the family and add to the family's problems. These feelings may cause family members to yell at each other and argue.

Breast Cancer and Teens

Having a mother with breast cancer can be especially hard on teens. Teens are at the age when they want to be more independent. Just at the time they're trying to separate themselves from home, their mother's breast cancer pulls them back in. They may have to take on more responsibilities at home. For example, they may have to help with housework or care for younger brothers and sisters. This leaves less time for friends and other activities and interests.

Ways to Cope

If you're a teen whose mother has breast cancer, you and your family may be in turmoil. Following are suggestions for how to cope as a family and as an individual.

> "When I found out my mom had breast cancer, I felt betrayed. Moms aren't supposed to get sick!"
> —Brian, age 16

Teen Talk

Ways to Cope as a Family

Try to encourage your family to do the following:

Have family meetings. Talk with each other about your feelings and concerns. Talk about what needs to be done and assign responsibilities.

Keep as normal a routine as possible. Have meals at regular times, do chores as usual, go to school and work, and have a set bedtime. Living and dealing with breast cancer can make you feel lost and uncertain. Having a routine gives you something to depend on.

Ask for help. Relatives, neighbors, and friends often want to help but may not know how. Ask for specific things you need, such as help with grocery shopping, laundry, child care, or rides to appointments.

Take breaks and have some fun. You will feel refreshed and better able to handle responsibilities.

Learn all you can about breast cancer. Knowing the facts can help you understand your mother's diagnosis and treatment. A great deal of information on breast cancer is available. The information at the back of this book contains many helpful resources.

Join a support group. Support groups for families dealing with cancer are available in many communities. Some are specifically for teens and children. Members of a support group share information and give each other ideas on ways to cope. You may not feel so alone when you see other families dealing with similar worries and fears.

Ways to Cope as an Individual

One important thing you can do is recognize your feelings and express them in a healthy way. You're likely to hurt yourself and others if you keep angry, scared feelings bottled up inside. Here are suggestions for dealing with your feelings in positive ways:

> **Let out your feelings by talking with someone who understands.** Talk with an adult family member, a school counselor, nurse, or spiritual advisor. There may be another teen in your school with a very sick parent. You might talk with this person, too.
>
> **If you feel yourself becoming angry, take a time-out and cool down.** Go for a walk, listen to music, or scream into a pillow. Try not to lash out at family members.
>
> **Control your mood swings by putting your feelings into words.** Write in a journal, talk into a tape recorder, or write a poem.
>
> **Ask your parents to tell you what's happening.** Tell them that not knowing makes you more scared than knowing.
>
> **Remember that it's all right to cry.** Find a safe time and place to let out your emotions.

Breast Cancer and Your Mother

A woman with breast cancer may become depressed, irritable, and impatient. Her family may get upset and angry because she's not acting like herself. Knowing about breast cancer's effects can help family members be more understanding.

Physically, a woman with breast cancer may be coping with fatigue and pain. Her cancer treatment may make her feel lousy or even violently ill. Most people have difficulty being upbeat and pleasant under such circumstances.

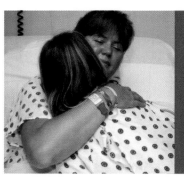

It's important to keep your mother involved in your life even if she's in the hospital.

Breast cancer has a great impact on a woman's emotions. For the first time, the woman may face the real possibility of dying. If she has lost a breast, she may feel less attractive. Hair loss, arm swelling, and weight loss or gain also can make her feel bad about herself. She may feel guilty because she's not able to help her family.

Ways to Help

If you're a teen whose mother has breast cancer, remember that you didn't cause your mother's illness. You don't have the power to make her well. You can, however, do things to make her feel more comfortable and lift her spirits. If your mother is in the hospital, here are ways you can help:

Decorate her room. Hospital rooms can seem cold and unfriendly. You can make your mother's surroundings more cheerful with family photos, plants and flowers, and homemade cards and banners.

Involve her in your life. When you visit, tell her about school and your friends. Show her your homework and ask for her help if she's up to it. Ask for her advice on any problems you may be having at school or home.

Help her pass the time. If she's feeling up to it, you can play a board game or talk about family history. Help her write thank-you notes. Bring books, magazines, and music that she might enjoy.

Some teen girls whose mother has breast cancer worry that their mother has passed cancer along to them. These teens and their mother share a genetic heritage. This means they may be at risk for developing cancer. It doesn't mean they automatically will get cancer. It's important for these teens to follow guidelines for early detection.

If your mother is recovering at home or undergoing treatment, here are ways you can help:

Anticipate her needs. Bring her snacks, a glass of water, or the newspaper. Adjust her pillow and blankets. Make sure she's not too warm or too cold.

Be considerate. Keep the volume on the TV or radio low. Ask before you invite friends over. Let her know when you're going out and when you'll be back.

Keep your house or apartment picked up (at least the part your mother can see). Sometimes, people feel more at ease when the home is clean and tidy.

Volunteer to run errands or take care of younger brothers and sisters.

Talk with your mother. Tell your mother how you're feeling. Let her express her feelings as well. Don't avoid your mother or shut yourself off from her.

Losing the Fight

Sometimes, even though she may get the best medical treatment, a woman may lose her battle against breast cancer. She may become too ill for the family to care for on their own. Nurses may come to the home to help the family. The mother may have to go to a hospital, nursing home, or hospice. A hospice is a special place that cares for dying people.

A mother's death from breast cancer may bring feelings of pain and sadness. Knowing that her suffering is over may bring relief.

If your mother is dying of breast cancer, her appearance and personality may change. She may moan or make unusual sounds and movements. There may be a strange smell. Despite these changes, your mother is the same person inside her body. She's the same woman who loves you. Let your mother know you love her.

You may feel a sense of relief at your mother's death because you know her suffering has ended. You also will feel a great deal of pain and sadness. Remember that life will continue, and someday you will feel happy again. Your pain will lessen, but your love for your mother will remain.

"My mother battled breast cancer for eight years. We thought the disease was gone, but then a new tumor was discovered on her spine. She spent one month in the hospital. A week before she was supposed to come home, she got pneumonia. Her body was just too weak to fight any longer. She died with our family by her side. I'll always be grateful that I got a chance to say good-bye."

Alison, Age 14

Points to Consider

How might dealing with a mother's breast cancer make a teen a stronger person?

How would you explain breast cancer to a younger sister or brother?

How could you help a friend whose mother has breast cancer?

Chapter Overview

Breast cancer among teens is rare. Teens, however, still should be concerned about this disease.

Teens can act now to lower their risk of breast cancer when they get older. They can lead a healthy lifestyle, practice monthly breast self-exams, and be activists for breast cancer.

A high-fat diet, smoking, drinking alcohol, and stress are thought to be risk factors for breast cancer. Lack of exercise also may increase a teen's chances of breast cancer.

A breast self-exam is done lying down, standing up, and before a mirror.

Many women and men have joined the fight against breast cancer. Teens also can join the breast cancer movement.

Chapter 6

Teens and Breast Cancer

It's extremely unlikely that a teen will develop breast cancer. The chance of a woman younger than age 25 developing breast cancer is 1 in 21,441. This is according to the American Cancer Society. However, teens still should be concerned about this disease. Teens can act now to lower their risk of breast cancer when they get older.

Lead a Healthy Lifestyle

Establishing good health habits as a teen may lower your risk of breast cancer as an adult. A link between a healthy lifestyle and breast cancer hasn't been proven for certain. Even if no connection exists, you still benefit by practicing the good health habits listed on the next page.

At a Glance

One recent study included young women whose mother or sisters had breast cancer. The study showed that eating vegetables and fruits may help such young women. Some of the young women ate five or more servings of vegetables and fruits a day. These women had a **70 percent** lower risk for breast cancer than those who ate fewer than two servings. Researchers recommend foods high in:

- Vitamin A (such as spinach and sweet potatoes)
- Vitamin C (kiwis, citrus, other fruits)
- Vitamin E (nuts, seeds)
- Beta carotene, which helps give some fruits and vegetables their color (carrots, cantaloupe, and peaches)

Exercise at least four hours each week.

Eat less food high in fat such as hamburgers and French fries and eat more fruits and vegetables instead.

Don't smoke.

Avoid stress.

Stay away from alcohol.

Do Breast Self-Exams

Breast self-exams (BSEs) are recommended for women age 20 and over. But it's a good idea for teens to do them, too. Starting as a teen can help you make BSEs a lifelong habit. You'll become familiar with your breasts and know what's normal for you. This can help you recognize changes. Doing BSEs may set a good example for your female relatives.

When to Do a Breast Self-Exam

The best time for a female to do a BSE is right after her period. (Specifically, this is five to seven days after the first day of her period.) At this time, the breasts are the least lumpy and aren't tender or swollen. Some girls don't have regular periods. These girls, as well as boys, can do a BSE on the same day every month.

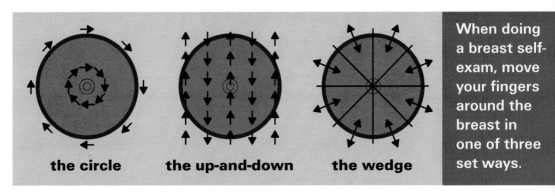

the circle   **the up-and-down**   **the wedge**

When doing a breast self-exam, move your fingers around the breast in one of three set ways.

How to Do a Breast Self-Exam

A breast self-exam is done in three parts: lying down, standing up, and before a mirror. If you have any questions about the right way to do an exam, ask a doctor.

Lying Down

1. Lie down and put a pillow or folded towel under your right shoulder. Place your right arm behind your head. This spreads the breast tissue evenly over your chest.

2. Use the finger pads of your three middle fingers on your left hand to feel for lumps or thickening in your right breast. Your finger pads are the top third of each finger. Keep your fingers flat.

3. Press firmly enough to know how your breast feels.

4. Move around the breast in a set way. You can choose either the circle, the up-and-down, or the wedge method. (See the above illustration.) Do it the same way every time. It will help you to make sure that you've gone over the entire breast area. Don't lift your fingers off the breast until the whole breast is examined. In the exam, include your underarm and the area up to the collarbone and below your breast.

5. Put the pillow or folded towel under your left shoulder. Examine your left breast using the finger pads of your right hand.

Encouraging family members and friends to do regular breast self-exams is one way to be a breast cancer activist.

Standing Up

Repeat the exam while standing with one arm behind your head. Standing up makes it easier to check the upper and outer part of the breasts (area toward your armpit). You may want to do this part of the BSE while you're in the shower. Some breast changes can be felt more easily when the skin is wet and soapy. Your hands can glide more easily, too.

Before a Mirror

1. Look at your breasts with your arms at your sides. Look for changes in shape or size of your breasts. Look for dimpling of the skin, changes in the nipple, redness, or swelling.

2. Next raise your arms high over your head. Look for the same types of changes listed in step one.

3. Place your hands on your hips and press down firmly to flex your chest muscles. Be aware that your right and left breasts won't match exactly. Again, look for changes.

Be an Activist

An activist is someone who works hard for a cause. Activists draw public attention to an issue or a problem and try to bring about change. Much of the progress in the fight against breast cancer has resulted from the work of activists. Women and men have spoken out about the need for more research on breast cancer. They have asked for early detection and better treatment methods.

The breast cancer movement needs teens to join in as well as adults. By becoming an activist for breast cancer, you can help yourself and others. Breast cancer is a major health problem for your parents' generation. Fighting breast cancer now may defeat its impact on your generation.

Here are ways you and other teens can be activists for breast cancer:

Learn all you can about breast cancer and tell others.

Encourage relatives and friends to do regular BSEs.

Help raise funds for breast cancer research and education.

Do clerical work for a local breast cancer organization.

Show support by wearing a pink ribbon, which is the symbol for breast cancer.

Write letters to lawmakers and other officials, asking for free or reduced-cost mammograms for women with low income.

"My buddies and I ran in Race for the Cure. **Mike, Age 16** We did it to show support for our friend Will. His mom's got breast cancer. We each paid to be in the race and bought T-shirts and caps. All the money goes to help fight breast cancer. You don't even have to run. You can just walk. A lot of people took part—it was great."

Points to Consider

Ask a relative if he or she does regular breast self-exams and why or why not.

How could you raise awareness in your school about breast cancer?

What are some ways a person with breast cancer could cope?

Chapter Overview

Better methods of detection and treatment are increasing the survival rates for women with breast cancer.

Helpful detection methods include MRI, PET scan, scintimammography, and T-scan. Gene testing and ductal lavage are other new detection methods. Sentinel node biopsy is a detection method that affects treatment.

More effective anticancer drugs are being developed. Bone marrow transplants may be another promising new treatment.

Some breast cancer activists want research to focus on finding the causes of the disease rather than on finding a cure.

Chapter 7

Looking Ahead

More women are surviving breast cancer than ever before. Improved ways of detecting and treating the disease are being introduced constantly. Someday breast cancer may be a manageable chronic illness such as diabetes or asthma. Everyone hopes that a cure, or cures, will be found. Because many types of breast cancer exist, more than one type of cure probably will be needed.

"When my dad and I found out about my mom's cancer, we got on the Internet right away. We found information about new treatments, and we got support from other families. Doing research like this helped us feel better. My dad said he and Mom felt like they were more in control and making their own decisions."

Malcolm, Age 15

Clinical trials are ways to test new therapies for humans. Clinical trials for cancer help evaluate possible treatments that seem to work in test tube or animal experiments. People with cancer may want to participate in clinical trials. If so, they should discuss this with their doctor.

Detecting Breast Cancer

Right now, mammography, clinical breast exams, and monthly breast self-exams are the best ways to detect breast cancer early. However, new imaging tools may improve doctors' ability to see inside the breast. The following techniques are in limited use today:

Magnetic resonance imaging (MRI). This technique uses a magnetic field and a special dye to light up tumors. MRI has been helpful in showing the extent of early breast cancers.

Positron emission tomography (PET scan). These scanners typically are used to map the brain but now are being used to help detect breast cancer. The woman receives a tiny amount of a radioactive drug. Images form based on the radioactivity the woman gives off after getting the drug. The PET scan maps these images. A PET scan may be helpful in examining women with very dense breast tissue. It also may let doctors know how well a patient with advanced breast cancer is responding to treatment.

Scintimammography. This technique uses a radioactive material and a special camera to reveal tumors. It's being used for tumors that can be felt but that don't show up on mammograms or ultrasounds.

T-scan. This device uses electricity to highlight tumors. If a mammogram or an ultrasound is unclear, a T-scan can help a doctor decide if a biopsy is needed.

Gene testing can detect if a woman has faulty breast cancer genes.

Gene Testing

Tests are becoming available to detect whether a woman has defective breast cancer genes. A woman who has these damaged genes then can begin treatment to prevent the disease. For example, she might start taking tamoxifen or another anticancer drug, or she might have a preventive mastectomy. Someday it may be possible to correct faulty genes through gene therapy.

Currently, genetic testing is expensive. Only the 5 to 10 percent of women genetically at risk for breast cancer benefit from the tests. Gene testing also can create some difficult situations. For example, a woman at high risk for breast cancer may be unable to get health insurance. She might face discrimination, or prejudice, in employment and other areas.

Ductal Lavage

Ductal lavage involves using mild suction to draw fluid from the nipple. Ducts that produce a drop of fluid are then washed with a saltwater solution. The cells washed out with this fluid are collected and studied. This test isn't meant to replace mammography or breast self-exams. Instead, it may help diagnose women who are at high risk for cancer or who have cancer in one breast. These ductal cells also may help researchers. They may show the relationship between the environment and breast cancer, as well as between genes and breast cancer.

Sentinel Node Biopsy

Sentinel node biopsy is part of the diagnostic process that affects treatment. In a sentinel node biopsy, surgeons inject a radioactive substance or dye. This substance or dye finds the one or two lymph nodes that drain a tumor. Surgeons then remove these sentinel, or guard, nodes and examine them for cancer. If the sentinel nodes are cancer-free, then no more nodes have to be removed. Sentinel node biopsy reduces the amount of surgery the woman needs. It also helps to prevent lymphedema.

Treating Breast Cancer

Surgery, chemotherapy, and radiation therapy probably will remain the main methods for treating breast cancer in the near future. However, promising new methods are being explored. These include the drug Herceptin, antiangiogenesis drugs, and bone marrow transplants.

Herceptin

Herceptin is a so-called smart drug. It targets only cancer cells. Unlike chemotherapy, Herceptin leaves healthy cells alone. At present, Herceptin is effective only for women who have tumors of a certain chemical makeup.

Antiangiogenesis Drugs

Antiangiogenesis drugs are being tested. These drugs are intended to cut off the tumor's blood supply. Without blood, the tumor can't survive and spread.

Bone Marrow Transplants

Studies using bone marrow transplants to treat cancer have had mixed results. Bone marrow is the spongy part of bones that produces blood cells. Bone marrow transplants may hold promise but more research needs to be done.

Breast Cancer

Researchers predict that sentinel node biopsies soon will become widely used.

A bone marrow transplant involves taking healthy cells from the woman's bone marrow. Then, she gets huge doses of chemotherapy drugs. After that, doctors inject the bone marrow cells back into the woman. The idea is to kill off the cancer cells. This allows the healthy cells to have a chance to grow and divide.

Finding the Causes of Breast Cancer

Some breast cancer activists believe that more effort should be put toward finding the causes of breast cancer. In particular, they want more research on the link between environmental pollution and breast cancer. According to this point of view, research efforts should answer questions such as the following. Which of the thousands of chemicals in the environment cause breast cancer and how? How are people exposed to these chemicals? Are there certain times, such as during breast development, when exposure is more dangerous than at other times?

Points to Consider

Would you participate in tests for a new breast cancer treatment? Why or why not?

Imagine that gene testing reveals you're going to develop a serious disease for which no cure is available. Would you want to know? Why or why not?

How might researchers go about finding an environmental cause for breast cancer?

Glossary

benign (bi-NINE)—not cancerous; a tumor that doesn't threaten life.

biopsy (BYE-op-see)—removal and examination of fluid and tissue from the living body; doctors perform biopsies to aid in diagnosis.

hormone (HOR-mohn)—a chemical in the body that controls growth, sexual development, and body functions

lumpectomy (luhm-PEK-tuh-mee)—surgery to remove a breast tumor and a limited amount of surrounding tissue

lymphedema (lim-fuh-DEE-mah)—swelling of the chest, arm, and hand caused by surgical removal of the lymph nodes under the arm

malignant (muh-LIG-nuhnt)—cancerous; a malignant tumor can be life threatening.

mammography (ma-MAW-gruh-fee)—X-ray examination of the breasts

mastectomy (ma-STEK-tuh-mee)—surgery to remove the breast

menstruation (men-stroo-AYE-shuhn)—the monthly discharge of blood, fluids, and tissue from the uterus in nonpregnant females

metastasis (muh-TASS-tuh-suhss)—the spread of cancer cells from their original location to other parts of the body

oncologist (ahn-KAH-luh-jist)—a doctor who specializes in diagnosing and treating cancer

prosthesis (prahss-THEE-suhss)—an artificial breast form

radiation (ray-dee-AY-shuhn)—energy that spreads out from a source such as radium

tumor (TOO-mur)—a mass of cells that isn't normal; a tumor may be a lump or a thickening of body tissue.

For More Information

Ingram, Carolyn, and Leslie Ingram Gebhart. *The Not-so-Scary Breast Cancer Book: Two Sisters' Guide From Discovery to Recovery.* Atascadero, CA: Impact Publishers, 2000.

Jordheim, Anne E. *What Every Young Person Should Know About Cancer.* Kettering, OH: PPI Publishing, 1997.

Kuehn, Eileen. *Death: Coping With the Pain.* Mankato, MN: Capstone, 2001.

Majure, Janet. *Breast Cancer.* Berkeley Heights, NJ: Enslow, 2000.

Nielsen, Jerri, and Maryanne Vollers. *Ice Bound: A Doctor's Incredible Battle for Survival at the South Pole.* New York: Hyperion, 2001.

Vogel, Carole G. *Will I Get Breast Cancer?: Questions and Answers for Teenage Girls.* Morristown, NJ: Julian Messner, 1995.

 At publication, all resources listed here were accurate and appropriate to the topics covered in this book. Addresses and phone numbers may change. When visiting Internet sites and links, use good judgment. Remember, never give personal information over the Internet.

Useful Addresses and Internet Sites

The Breast Cancer Fund
2107 O'Farrell
San Francisco, CA 94115-3419
1-866-760-8223
www.breastcancerfund.org

Breast Cancer Society of Canada
401 St. Clair Street
Point Edward, ON N7V 1P2
CANADA
1-800-567-8767
www.bcsc.ca

National Alliance of Breast Cancer
Organizations (NABCO)
9 East 37th Street, 10th Floor
New York, NY 10016
1-888-80-NABCO (888-806-2226)
www.nabco.org

Susan G. Komen Breast Cancer Foundation
5005 LBJ Freeway, Suite 250
Dallas, TX 75244
1-800-I'M AWARE (800-462-9273)
www.breastcancerinfo.com

Y-ME National Breast Cancer Organization
212 West Van Buren Street, Fifth Floor
Chicago, IL 60607
1-800-221-2141
www.y-me.org

American Cancer Society
www.cancer.org
Contains information on all types of cancer
www3.cancer.org/cancerinfo/load_cont.asp?ct
=28&language=english
Provides answers to frequently asked questions
about male breast cancer

Cancer Survivors Network
www.acscsn.org
Offers a discussion board, links to personal
web pages, and even an expression gallery

Girl Scouts of America
http://jfg.girlscouts.org/talk/whoami/issues/
breastcancer.htm
Helps teens to learn and speak about breast
cancer

National Cancer Institute
www.nci.nih.gov
Has information on types of cancer,
treatments, clinical trials, and more

National Cancer Institute
Cancer Information Service
1-800-4-CANCER (800-422-6237)

Y-ME National Breast Cancer Organization
"Just for Teens" program
1-800-221-2141

Index

Index continued